MODERN TOSS PRESENTS

First published 2018 by Modern Toss Ltd.
Modern Toss, PO Box 386, Brighton BN1 3SN, England
www.moderntoss.com

ISBN 978-0-9929107-7-8

Text and illustrations copyright © Modern Toss Limited, 2018
PO Box 386, Brighton BN1 3SN, England

A CIP catalogue record for this book is available from the British Library.

Designed and typeset by Modern Toss
Printed and bound by TJ International

Visit www.moderntoss.com to read more about all our books and to buy them yeah.
You will also find lots of other shit there, and you can sign up to our mailing list so
that you're always kept bang up to date with it, cheers.

Tossary of Terms

A GLOSSARY OF TERMS FOR POINTLESS MODERN PHENOMENA

by Jon Link & Mick Bunnage

scumcestor

[skuhm-ses-ter]

An unwelcome discovery in your family tree.

- *She could trace her scumcestors back to some bloke who was hanged for mass murder in France.*
- *Your scumcestral heritage explains why your dad is such an arsehole.*

screen margarine

[skreen mahr-juh-reen]

The build-up of face and ear grease on a smartphone screen.

preating

[pree-ting]

Dramatically slashing the cost of
an expensive meal by eating a loaf
of bread before you go out.

- *Pop round ours for some preats
before we hit the restaurant, yeah?*

prioritit

[prihy-or-i-tit]

Paying a bit extra to get on the plane before everyone else.

- *The man in the Panama hat used his prioritit status to
assert dominance within the budget traveller hierarchy.*

nocturnal cunt horn

[nok-tur-nl kuhnt-hawn]

A car alarm that goes off in the middle of the night.

- *Hello, is that the police? Yeah, I've got a nocturnal cunt horn going off outside me house.*

chillaxative

[chil-lak-suh-tiv]

Deliberately listening to pan pipe music till you shit yourself.

button clutterist

[buht-n kluht-er-ist]
Half-arsedly typing misspelt words into Google
in the hope it'll make sense of it for you.

nose bark

[noze bahrk]
An unexpected violent sneeze that
makes everyone jump.

yawnweaver

[yawn-wee-ver]

A long-form storyteller, often specialising
in extended dull travel anecdotes.

thumbxiety

[thum-zahy-i-tee]

Anxious tension created by
not wanting to be the one to
end a text conversation.

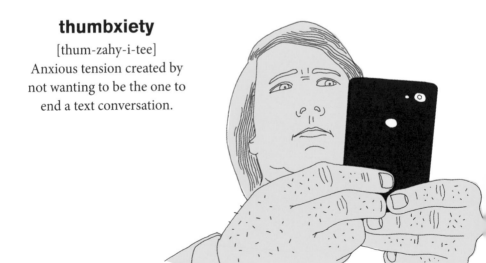

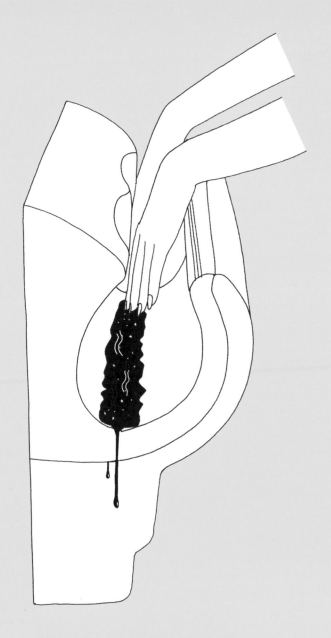

Attenborough's trench

[aht-n-buhr-oh-z trench]
DNA bacterial soup cultivating in
a blade hand dryer trough.

dickory dock

[dik-uh-ree dok]
A gentrified urban canalside area with expensive
nik-nak shops and stalls selling South American bread.

Holby bolter

[hohl-bee bohl-ter]
Racing to switch the channel
before you hear the theme tune to
a programme you can't stand.
*e.g. The Archers, Panorama, party
political broadcasts.*

We've run out of AA batteries so I put a potato in.

shitstitution
[shit-sti-tyoot-shun]
Getting a supermarket home delivery
substitution that's so way off it's mental.

blue-sky drinking
[bloo-skihy drin-king]
Doing a litre of scotch in the toilets to loosen
up for a marketing ideas meeting.

thickularity

[thik-u-lar-i-tee]
When society collectively reaches
the point where it has become too
stupid to function.

UUUUUUURRGGGGGGGGGGGGGHHHHHHHHHHHHHHHHHHHHHHHHFUCKSAKE...

afteryawn

[af-ter-yawn]
Adding a phrase or swearword
onto the end of a long yawn.

combo harvester

[kom-boh hahr-vuh-ster]
Someone who can bang a meal deal down
really quickly during their lunch break.

scrotiniser

[skroh-tin-i-zuhr]
A dog that sticks its nose
into blokes' trousers.

13

back sack twat

[bak sak twaht]
Swinging a lump pack around
in a public space with all the
care and attention of a drunk
driving toff who's forgotten
he's towing a horsebox.

arseclamation mark
[ahrs-kluh-mey-shuh n mahrk]
A dog's arsehole that's on permanent
display due to its vertical tail.
- *Your dog's arseclamation mark has
put me right off this biscuit.*

rustlepang
[ruhs-uh l pang]
An inexplicably overwhelming desire to
eat food you don't even want, triggered
by the subliminal audio detection of
crinkling food packaging.

pavement shit parade

[peyv-muh-nt shit-puh-reyd]
Proud outdoor showcasing of the knackered contents of your
fucked up life instead of wasting effort taking it all up the dump.

cock bonnet

[kok bon-it]
Floppy men's cap
popularised by
TV series Peaky Blinders.

- *When we meet him later on I hope
he isn't wearing his cock bonnet.*

newmoania

[noo-moh-nee-uh]
Whingeing about the introduction of
anything fucking new. Highly contagious
among middle-aged men.

nob rule
[nob-ruh l]
When more than one
member of government
has been to Eton.
see also: **nobocracy**

Arthur Sixpence
[ahr-ther siks-puh ns]
A customer, born before the year 2000, who's made to feel like
he's trying to operate within some dubious feudal bartering
system by offering to pay for something with actual money.

mince trotters

[mins trot-ers]
A pair of loafers worn
without socks.

youlogy

[yoo-luh-jee]
Hijacking a celebrity death to promote or talk about yourself.
Often involves recounting a personal anecdote that over-stresses
your importance in their success story.

NICE LITTLE SHOP

serftopia

[surf-toh-pee-uh]
The dream of owning a little
shop or cafe and serving the
public, whilst simultaneously
ignoring the drudgery and
long hours that would
involve running it.

sit downer

[sit dou-ner]
Low mood triggered by
walking past a memorial
death bench in the park.

loiterature

[loi-ter-uh-cher]
Half-arsedly flicking through books you're not
going to buy in airport bookshops.

ambient muck-spreader

[am-bee-uhnt muhk-spred-er]

A person who plays a public-use piano in a train station.

- *I'm trying to top up my oyster card when this ambient muck-spreader fucks with my head like I'm eating croissants with Helena Bonham Carter.*

Kipling's smog
[kip-lings smog]
A massive cloud of cake-flavoured steam pumped out by someone using an electronic vaping device.

socketponce
[sok-it-pons]
Recharging your phone via someone else's electricity supply at every available opportunity.

tumour morsels

[tyoo-mer mawr-suh-lz]
Soft coloured sweets, often with smiley
faces, made from animal gut slurry.
- *We had a long drive to Cornwall, so
I stuffed me kids full of tumour morsels.*

tat rebater

[tat rey-beht-er]
Having the arse-tightening audacity
to consider taking something back to
the charity shop for a refund.

If you won't give me
a refund can I swap it for
a Phil Collins CD?

UUUUUUURRRRRRRRGGGGGGGGGGGGGGGGGGGHHHHHHHHHHHHHHHHH...

yawndice

[yawn-dis]

A nerve-jangling over-exuberant yawn, often delivered in the form of a verbalised three bar yodel, usually occurring during a crucial plot point of your favourite programme.

retinal perma-fresco

[ret-in-uh l purm-ah-fres-koh]

Seeing something that you didn't ask to see, but now can't forget, like being texted a photo of someone's cock by mistake.

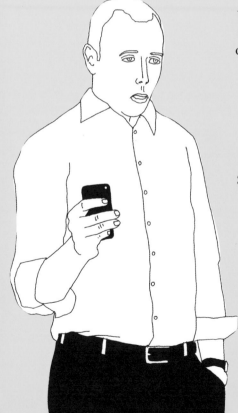

Alright mate, I'm in Goa yeah, who you down the pub with then?

fucket list

[fuhk-it list]

A meticulously kept list of stuff you can't be arsed to do before you die.

- *After listening to him banging on about Goa, I stuck it straight on my fucket list.*

(*see also:* parachute jump for charity, scuba diving off the Galapagos Islands, building a kit car)

triggercide

[trig-er-sahyd]
Curating your anger portfolio by actively searching out stuff to get really livid over.

bicwig

[bik-wig]
Hair tattoo for bald blokes.

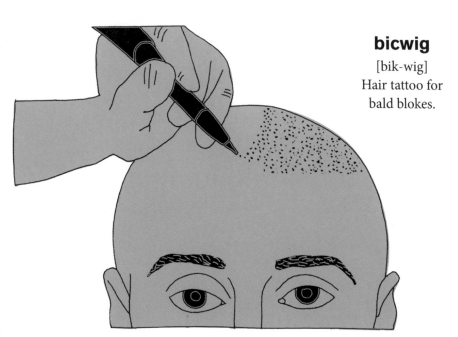

data barnacle

[dey-tuh bahr-nuh-kuh l]
Cafe customer who leeches four hours'
worth of free WiFi in exchange for shelling
out two quid on a cup of fruit tea.

ET's multi-storey finger

[ee-tees muhl-tee-stohr-ee fing-er]
The unbreachable distance between the tip
of your finger at full-stretch and the ticket
machine in a municipal car park.

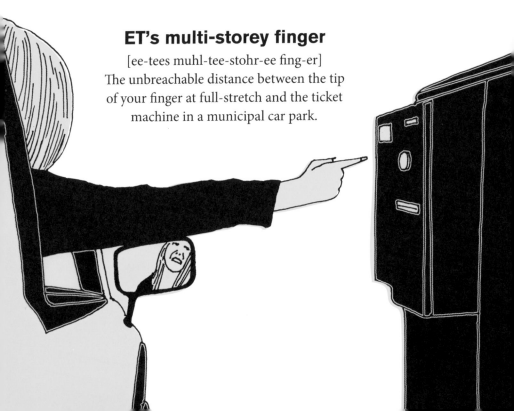

concrete freckle

[kon-kreet frek-uh l]
Flattened chewing gum bonded onto the pavement.

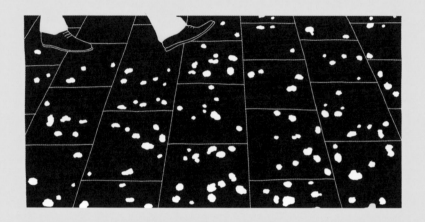

thespi-'avinyou

[thes-pee-hav-in-ya]
Sarcastic drama student working
reluctantly in a gastropub to pay the rent.

clump-nuggets

[kluhmp-nuhg-itz]

1. A small gathering of young people who hang out together in shopping centres.

2. A group of four or more chicken nuggets, frozen together in a lump over several months.

stinkquisition

[stingk-wuh-zish-uh n]

Catching a whiff of something you're not familiar with and following up with an interrogation.

One of you ladies been eating peanuts?

bleedophile
[bleed-duh-fahyl]
Some arsehole with
hi-frequency overspill
emanating from ill-fitting
headphones.

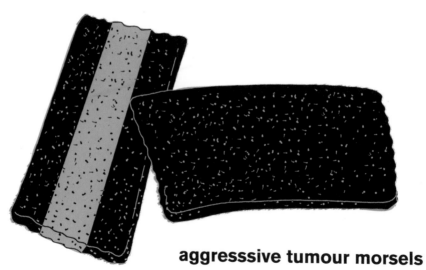

aggresssive tumour morsels
[uh-gres-iv tyoo-mer-mawr-suh-lz]
Tangy/sour-flavoured soft coloured sweets,
usually more abstract in shape than the
standard tumour morsel.

entersplainer

[en-ter-spleyn-er]

Someone who actually knows how to do something constructive,
earning money filming themselves doing it instead of actually doing it.

▪ *He who can, monetises his own entersplainment channel.*
He who cannot, watches it.

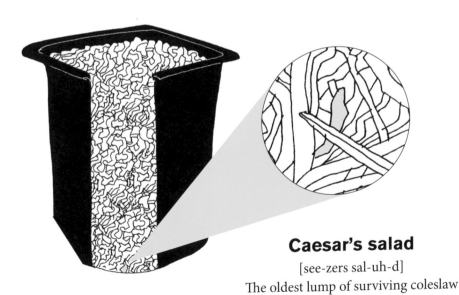

Caesar's salad

[see-zers sal-uh-d]

The oldest lump of surviving coleslaw
in an all-you-can-eat salad bar.

quirkjaculate

[kwurk-jak-yuh-leyt]
Short, intense meeting where employees
try to splurge ideas all over each other.

scalphetti

[skalp-et-ee]
A strand of hair found in a meal.

self quacknosis

[self kwak-noh-sis]
Attempting to identify the symptoms
of your illness on the internet.

oikacrat

[oik-a-krat]
Local criminal often recognised and celebrated
for getting arrested in a TV police clip show.

throat-revving

[throht-rev-ing]
Repetitive throat clearing
following a heavy cold.
Useful for breaking up long
boring sentences.

shitnak

[shit-nak]
Irresistable novelty impulse
purchase, currently propping up
several international economies.

▪ *The royal wedding ceramic
thimble has saved our shit-nak
company from going tits up down
the arsepipe.*

the invisibill man

[th-ee in-viz-uh-buhl man]
The futile act of trying to attract the
waiting staff's attention when you want
to settle up and leave.

sportsmoat

[spohrts-moht]

Avoiding the complications of the outside world by sealing yourself into a bubble of sport. If anything really important happens it will surely leak into the sports news.

Peter borough-ism

[pee-ter bur-oh-iz-uh-m]
The naming of children after the
place where they were conceived.

gloomjoyment

[gloom-joi-muh-nt]
Watching a really heavy dystopian drama as
chilled out evening entertainment.

smug goblet

[smuhg gob-lit]
The feeling you get using a re-usable cup, turning your flat white addiction into an eco-warrior statement and saving the planet one coffee at time.

bargaintography

[bahr-guh-n-tog-ruh-fee]
Blatantly photographing an item in a shop with the deliberate intent of going home and purchasing it online at a discount.

In the latter stages of the war people were eating the legs off dogs just to stay alive

adolf flipler

[a-dolf flip-lur]
Retaining dictator-style dominance over the remote control even though you're not even fucking watching the TV.

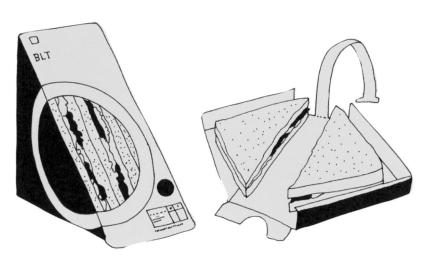

prawn cathedral

[pr-orhn kuh-thee-druhl]
Over-the-top paper engineering technology for showcasing a supermarket sandwich.

smog trotter
[smog trot-er]
An inner-city jogger who inhales large amounts of lead while trying to get fit.

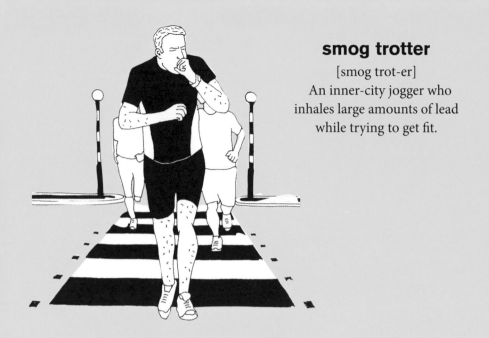

chatinoculation
[chat-ih-nok-yuh-ley-shuh n]
Going out of your way to make small talk with your neighbour early in the day so you don't have to go their house party later on.

What a lovely day, is that a new top you've got on?

He's obviously not planning on coming to my party tonight.

abstract expressionism
[ab-strakt ik-spresh-uh-niz-uh-m]
The almost wordless use of freestyle eye movements,
facial expressions and hand gestures to communicate
complex ideas and emotional states. A highly evolved
contemporary language system impenetrable to old school
verbal practitioners and traditional mouth merchants.

pisstal maze
[pis-tl meyz]
I need a piss but whoa, hang on, am I a cactus or a sombrero? These over-thought-out shithouse door graphics aren't helping. Now I'm busting. Sorry mate, turns out I was a clarinet, not a tambourine.

hum cushion
[huhm koo sh-uh-n]
Faint whiff of dog's arse on a neighbour's sofa or public transport seat.

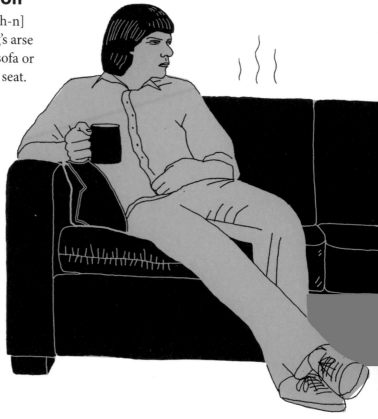

slothmosis

[slohth-moh-sis]

Buying a book or an app about how to
do something instead of actually doing it.
*e.g. how to tidy up, keep fit, learn to paint,
write code.*

bob blazer

[bob bley-zer]

Forgetting to switch off
your hair straighteners, then
leaving them on the bed
while you're down the pub.

signature dish
[sig-nuh-cher dish]
Adding your unique
personal DNA thumbprint
to a customer's meal by
sneezing into it.

slug pimping
[sluhg pim-ping]
Extreme over-customised
eyebrows.

network shit-throbber

[net-wurk shit-throb-er]
Migraine created by trying to compare complex rail journey ticket options.
▪ *Where's the nearest chemist? I've given myself a network shit-throbber trying to buy an off-peak travelcard.*

stilton hotel

[stil-tn hoh-tel]
Airbnb-ing a dirty room in your house.

Here's your room. If you get peckish, there's some leftover pizza by the side of the bed.

Packham's arse drizzler

[pak-uh-ms ahrs driz-ler]
A roosting bird that shits its guts out all
over a car parked under a tree.

blagpiper

[blahg-pi-per]
Wading in on a subject with your own hot take,
even though you know fuck-all about it.

pinkfield site

[pingk-feeld sahyt]
An area of clear skin ripe for inking in.
see also: **brownbelt site**

gizmo stroke

[giz-moh strohk]
Expensive hi-tech equipment
that stops working just after
the guarantee runs out.
see also: **giznitas** - the humane
death clinic for gadgets that have
just about had enough of it.

appointlessment

[uh-point-les-ment]

Stubbornly keeping a doctor's appointment you booked two weeks ago when you were ill, even though you now feel much better.

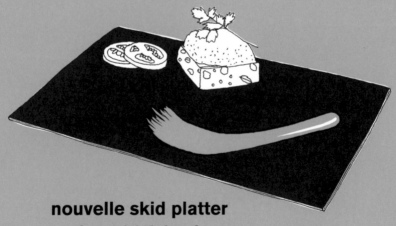

nouvelle skid platter

[noo-vel skid plat-er]

A smear of sauce on a plate of contemporary food, often served on waste building material.

- *I wanted my nouvelle skid platter arranged on a plate of slate, but it turned up on an unfinshed lump of wood which had soaked up the juices of previous meals.*

crispy swan

[kris-pee swon]
A towel sculpture made with a dirty towel.

And now, to get a different point of view on this latest rocket launch, we're going to talk to a flat earth expert...

FLAT EARTHER

NEWS LATEST ON SPACE X LAUNCH LIVE

DOW 12.498.46 GOOG 1,060.32 YHOO 41.44 DAX 12,761.38 ETC N THAT

the rational front

[th-uh rash-uh-nl fruhnt]
TV news programmes that go out of their way to create impartiality and balance in a debate by inviting some whacko on to give their slant on it.

vlogorrhoea

[vlog-uh-ree-uh]
A compulsive disorder characterised by filming everything you do from the moment you wake up.
see also: **diaryorrhoea**

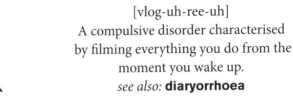

greedeemer

[greed-dee-mer]
Showing the waiter a voucher code on your phone before you order food in a restaurant.

verbal grouting

[vur-buhl grout-ing]

Padding out idea-thin statements with content-free supportive filler.

• *So, let me be clear, verbal grouting, it's like, really useful? If you, like, literally don't have anything to, like, say? Jagetmee?*

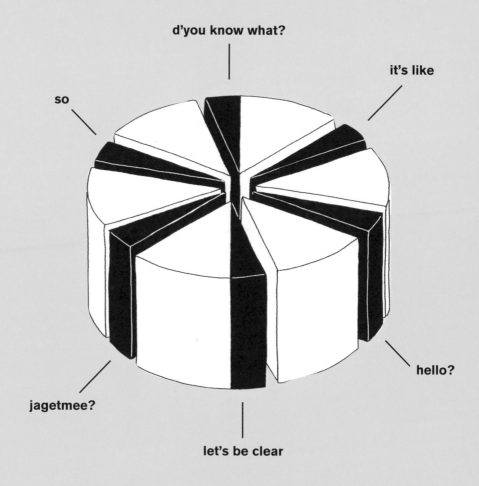

d'you know what?

it's like

so

jagetmee?

let's be clear

hello?

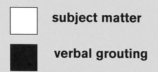

☐ **subject matter**

■ **verbal grouting**

apotalypse noodles
[uh-pot-uh-lips nood-l-s]
Stocking up on pot noodles in case of nuclear war.
If there's no water supply, use your own spit.
see also: **snackageddon** - the same basic
idea but with space-saving Pringles.

ghost milking

[gohst milk-ing]
An auto-renewing subscription
to something you never use.

direct doggit

[dih-rekt dog-it]
The money sapped from your bank
account by a professional dog walker.

breeder's logbook

[bree-ders log-book]
A book used to catalogue
the names of friends'
children's birthdays.

aggroffiti

[ag-roh-fee-tee]
An un-premeditated scream from the primal id.
Expressionist Pre-street-art style.

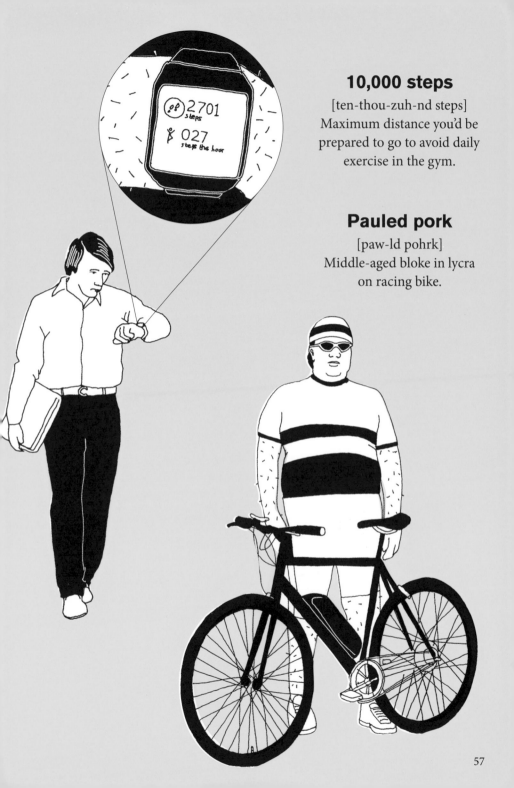

10,000 steps

[ten-thou-zuh-nd steps]
Maximum distance you'd be
prepared to go to avoid daily
exercise in the gym.

Pauled pork

[paw-ld pohrk]
Middle-aged bloke in lycra
on racing bike.

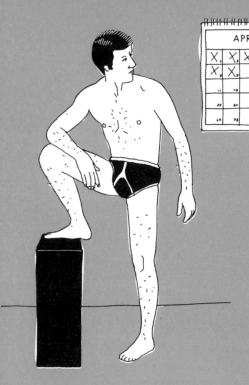

pantathalon
[pant-ath-a-lon]
Challenging personal-best
hygiene boundaries to see how long
you can get away with
wearing the same pair of pants.

smut shuttle
[smuht shuht-l]
Train carriage containing at least
one commuter watching Game of
Thrones sex scenes on a laptop.

D'you mind if I draw
the curtains? That
dragon staring at me
is putting me right off.

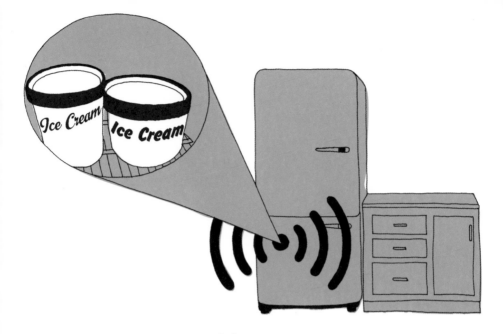

gut-beacon

[guht bee-kuh n]
Signal beamed directly to human stomach
from uneaten ice cream in freezer.

business thrush

[biz-nis thruhsh]
Picking up germs or an illness
from a shared hot desk.

- *A major business thrush
outbreak has been traced back to
an infected mouse mat.*

weblice

[weblihys]

Angry groups of online keyboard warriors,
individually harmless but capable of extreme
digital infestation when working as a swarm.

▪ *The typeface tweak we applied to our
traditional chocolate bar packaging attracted
an overwhelming weblice assault which resulted in
the complete collapse of our 100-year-old family
business and the laying off of all our staff.*

Basil's fuck yodel

[baz-uh-ls fuk yohd-l]
The unsettling sound of urban
foxes having it off at night.

wall stubble

[wawl stuhb-uh l]
Ghostly dirt surround that an
old picture leaves behind when
taken off the wall.

index